Series - *Children's Nature Quest*

Author

M Borhan

From

Big 6 Publishing

Why we need the sea?

The sea is a vital component of Earth's ecosystem, providing a home to an incredibly diverse array of marine life. It plays a crucial role in regulating the planet's climate by absorbing and redistributing heat. Additionally, the sea is a vital source of sustenance for billions of people, supplying a significant portion of the world's food and supporting economies through fisheries and trade.

For Ships
Ships, powered by massive engines, can cross oceans and are crucial for global trade, connecting distant ports and transporting goods around the world.

Do you know the Titanic?
The Titanic, a marvel of early 20th-century engineering, was the largest and most luxurious ship of its time. On its ill-fated Maiden voyage in 1912, it tragically collided with an iceberg and sank, claiming over 1,500 lives. Despite its state-of-the-art safety features, the sinking of the Titanic remains one of the most infamous maritime disasters in history, sparking changes in maritime regulations and capturing the world's collective imagination.

Resourceful SEASHORE
The seashore is a dynamic ecosystem where land and sea meet, providing habitats for a variety of organisms, and it experiences changing tides that influence its biodiversity.

The STARFISH
Starfish, or sea stars, have a remarkable ability to regenerate lost arms, and some species can even grow a new body from a single arm and part of the central disc.

Seals, highly adapted to aquatic life, can close their nostrils and remain submerged for long periods, and some species possess remarkable diving abilities, reaching depths of hundreds of meters.

PENGUINS
Penguins, flightless birds, are exceptional swimmers using their wings as flippers, and they often form large colonies, displaying complex social behaviors.

Time for Diving !

Diving is a captivating underwater activity that allows individuals to explore the mesmerizing depths of the ocean, encountering vibrant marine life and discovering hidden underwater landscapes. Whether for recreation, scientific research, or professional purposes, diving offers a unique and immersive experience beneath the sea's surface.

Let's Dive Deep....
Let's dive deep into the unknown, where sunlight fades, and the mysterious ocean depths unfold, revealing a world of bioluminescent wonders and extraordinary marine biodiversity. As we plunge into the Blue, the silent currents and vibrant ecosystems beckon, inviting us to explore secrets concealed beneath the surface.

Sea Anemones
They are marine animals that attach to substrates on the ocean floor and have a tubular body with tentacles surrounding a central mouth.

SEA FISH
The diversity of sea fish is immense, ranging from tiny colorful reef fish to massive oceanic species, contributing significantly to global fisheries and diets.

DOLPHIN

Dolphins, highly social marine mammals, use echolocation for navigation and communication, and they exhibit playful behaviors, often riding the blow waves of boats.

OCTOPUS
Octopuses, highly intelligent marine animals, have complex nervous systems and can change color and texture to camouflage, expressing remarkable adaptability.

CORALS
Coral reefs, built by tiny coral polyps, are vital marine ecosystems, supporting diverse marine life, and they face threats from climate change and human activities.

TORTOISE

Sea turtles, often referred to as sea tortoises, have a remarkable navigational ability, returning to the same beaches where they were born to lay their eggs.

Sunrise over the sea is a serene and tranquil moment, marking the beginning of a new day with the gradual emergence of light from the eastern horizon.

Amazing SUNSET

Sunsets at sea create stunning displays of color as the sun dips below the horizon, with the ocean reflecting hues of red, orange, and pink, creating a mesmerizing spectacle.

SURFING

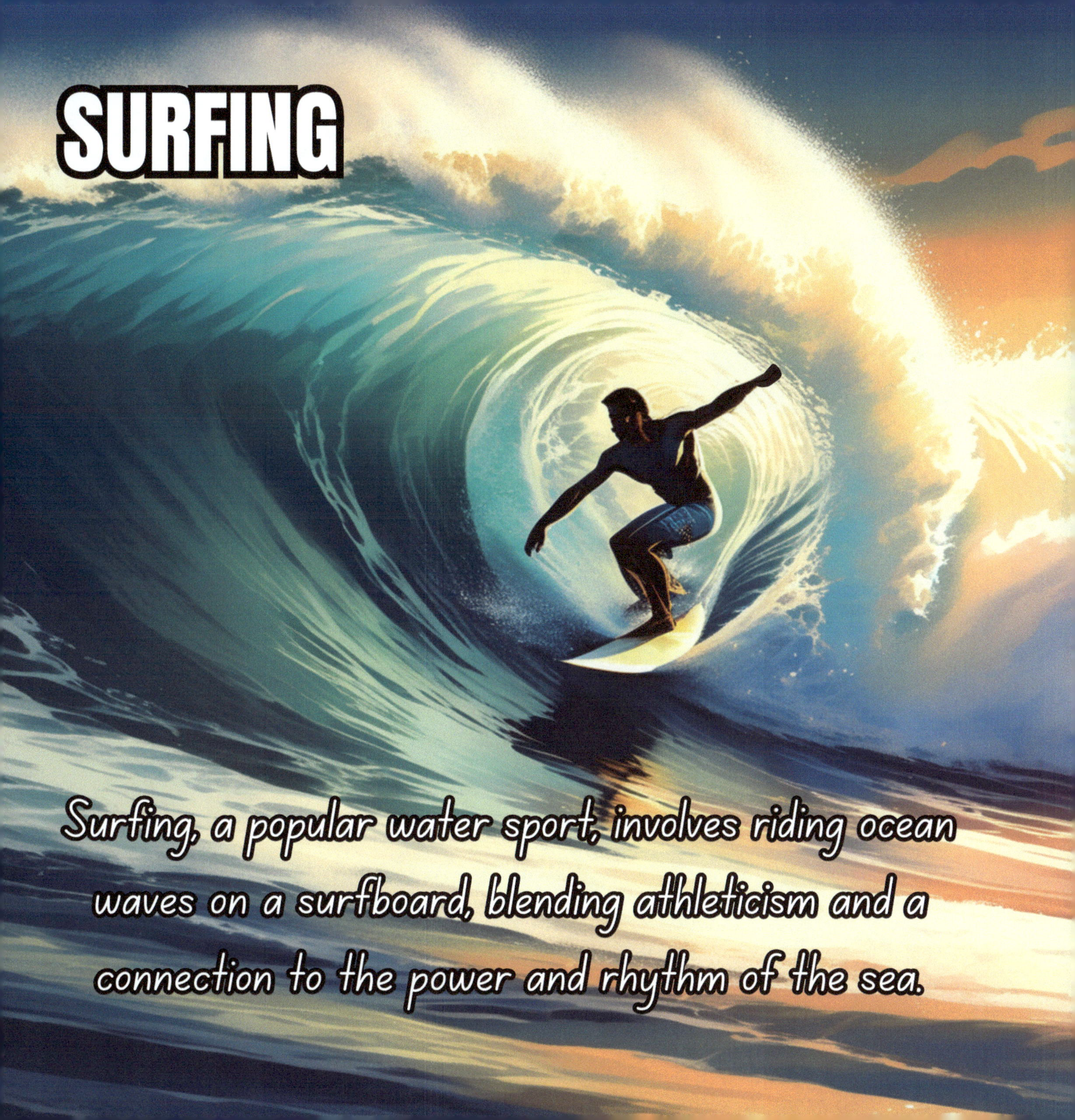

Surfing, a popular water sport, involves riding ocean waves on a surfboard, blending athleticism and a connection to the power and rhythm of the sea.

Exploring the sea is a thrilling adventure where one delves into the mysteries of the underwater world, encountering diverse marine life and discovering the beauty hidden beneath the waves. With each dive, one becomes a witness to the mesmerizing landscapes and wonders that the ocean holds.

Grab Other Exciting Books

Book Series: Children's Knowledge Quest

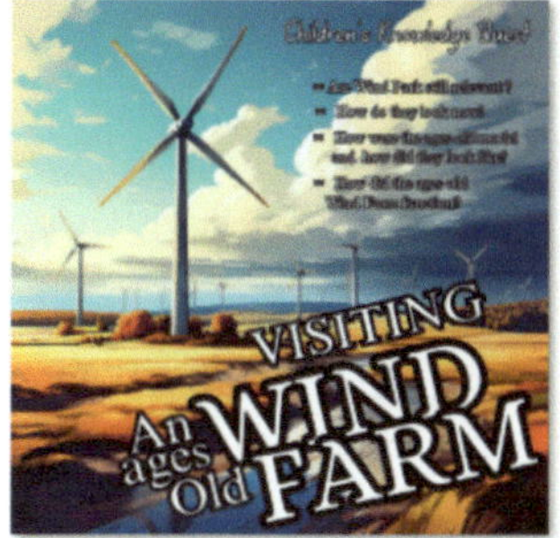

Book Series: Grizzly Bear Series

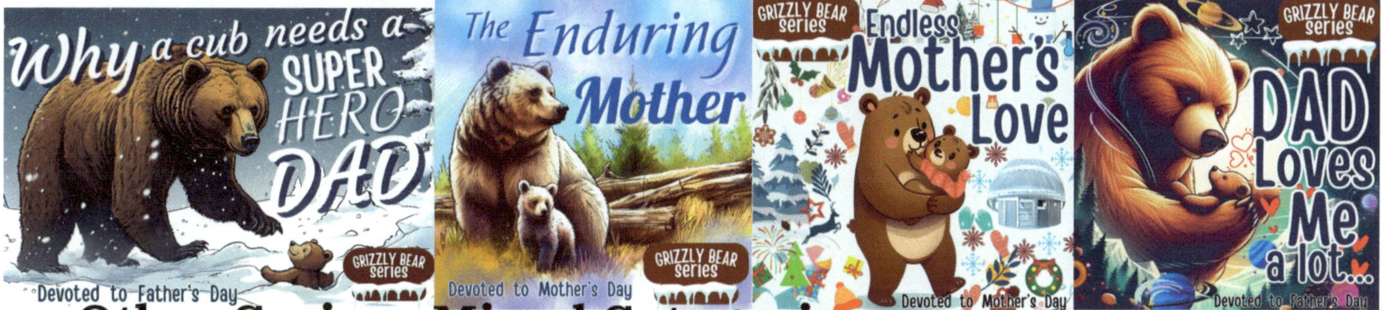

Other Series: Mixed Categories

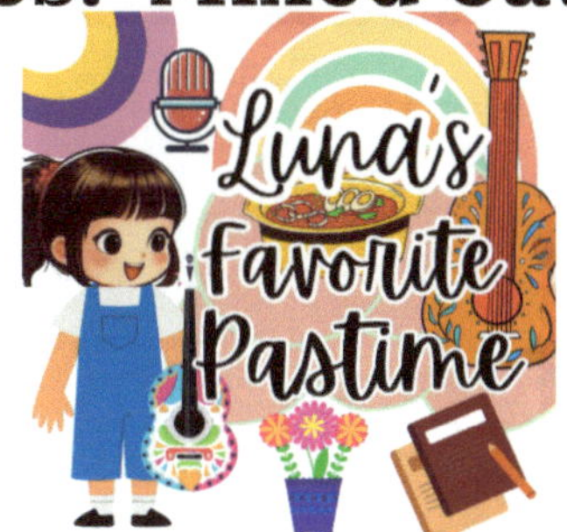

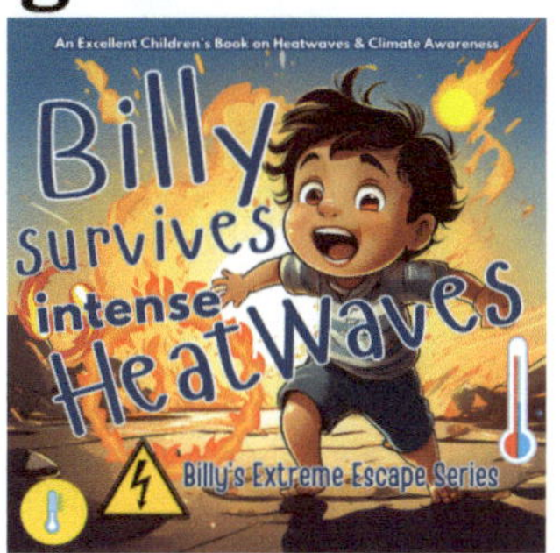

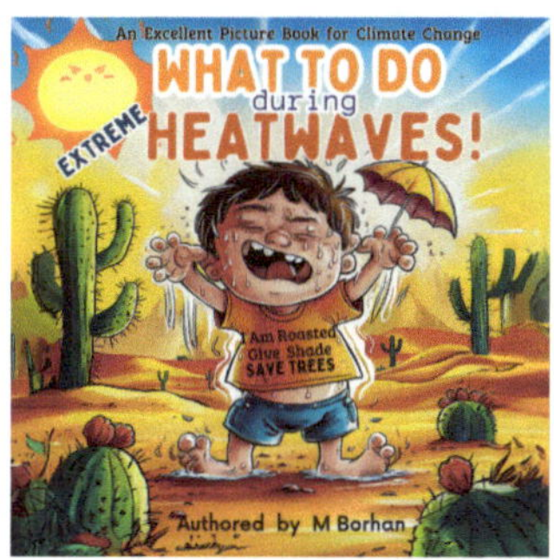

Instagram

Scan QRs, Follow & Like us

Pinterest

Tiktok